WHAT'S THE BIG IDEA?

The Mind

Nicola Barber
Illustrated by Ross Collins

Hodder
Children's
Books

a division of Hodder Headline plc

What's the Big Idea? focuses on the hottest issues and ideas around. In a nationwide survey, we asked young people like you to tell us which subjects you find most intriguing, worrying and exciting.
The books in this series tell you what you need to know about the top-rated topics.

Books available now:
The Mind
Virtual Reality
Women's Rights

Books coming soon:
Animal Rights
The Environment
Religion
Time and the Universe

We would love to hear what you think. If you would like to make any comments on this book or suggestions for future titles, please write to us at:

What's the Big Idea?
Hodder Children's Books
338 Euston Road
London NW1 3BH

This book is dedicated to Patrick – a fine mind.

*The publishers would like to thank
Maureen Horner BA C Psychol
for her expert advice.*

Contents

Welcome to the search for the mind 6

Journey to the centre of the brain 14

Studying the mind 30

Thanks for the memory 46

Seeing is believing 58

Learning and intelligence 70

What makes you 'you' 86

The mind asleep 92

Animal minds 96

Mind mysteries 104

The future of the mind 108

Further reading 121

Great minds in the history of the mind 122

Glossary 125

Index 127

Welcome to the Search for THE MIND

Have you ever stopped to think just how truly astounding you are? Well, let's try it now. What have you done since you got out of bed this morning?

thought a few thoughts

brushed your teeth

played a computer game

eaten some breakfast

read a book

ridden your bike

But how do you know how to do all of these things? Even brushing your teeth is an amazing feat of recognition and recall.

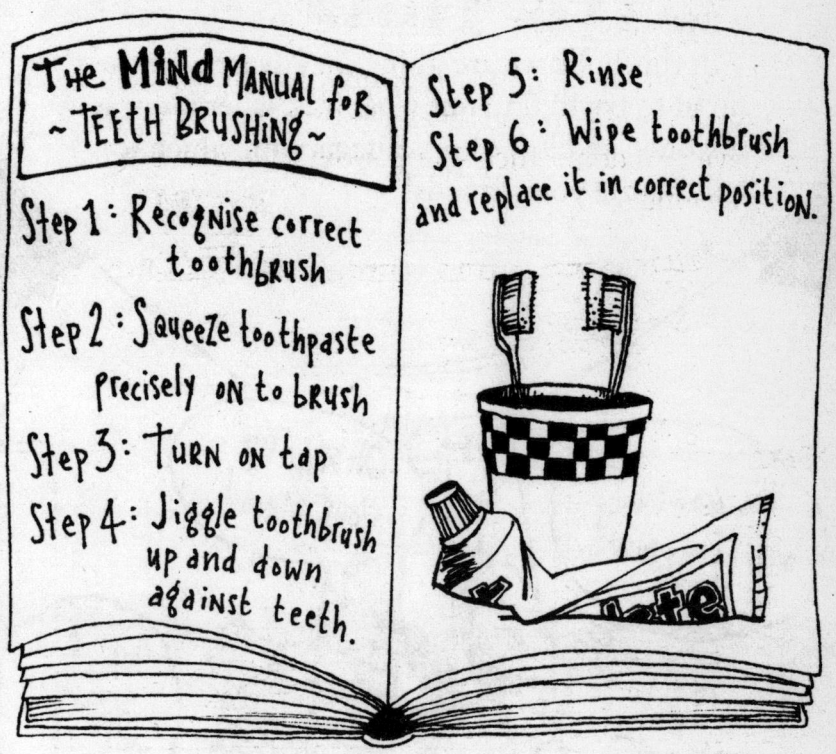

The **Mind** Manual for ~ TEETH Brushing ~

Step 1: Recognise correct toothbrush

Step 2: Squeeze toothpaste precisely on to brush

Step 3: Turn on tap

Step 4: Jiggle toothbrush up and down against teeth.

Step 5: Rinse

Step 6: Wipe toothbrush and replace it in correct position.

The miracle of the human mind is that as you stand in front of the bathroom sink you don't even have to think about all these separate steps. You have learned how to brush your teeth, and your amazing mind stores that knowledge.

OK, so I am an amazing, talented, wonderful human miracle! But the BIG question is: what is this thing called 'mind' which makes me such a star?

In this book we are going on a search for the mind to try to find out what it is, where it is, how it works, and lots of other facts with which to bamboozle your friends!

You can see from all these sayings that the word 'mind' can mean all sorts of different things – memory, an intention to do something, the place where thinking happens, the seat of intelligence.

Our search for the mind will take us through all these different aspects – and a few more you might not have thought of.

Where is the mind? This question has vexed even the cleverest people for centuries!

The first great debate was whether the mind is in the heart or in the head. The Ancient Egyptians thought that the heart was the centre of human life. They said that the heart recorded all the good and evil deeds done in a person's life. They believed that when someone died, the gods weighed their heart against a feather to see if it was heavy with guilt, or light and free from sin.

Before embalming a body to preserve it, the Ancient Egyptians scooped out the brain through the nostrils and threw it away. So they obviously didn't think that the brain was very important.

Early Greek thinkers also saw the heart as the most important organ in the body.
Then along came Hippocrates (460-370 BC) …

MEN OUGHT TO KNOW THAT FROM NOTHING ELSE BUT THE BRAIN COME JOYS DELIGHTS, LAUGHTER AND SPORT, AND SORROWS, GRIEFS DESPONDENCY AND LAMENTATION…

YOU'RE A NUTTER

Despite Hippocrates' words, the debate continued for centuries. Even today we still associate the heart with the emotions and even sometimes with memory. For instance, we say things like, 'She's broken my heart!' or 'I've got to learn this poem off by heart.'

Even when philosophers decided that it was probably the brain, rather than the heart, that was responsible for mental functions, that wasn't the end of the matter.

René Descartes (1596-1650), a French philosopher who liked to lie in bed all morning reading and thinking, came to the conclusion that the mind and the body were entirely separate from each other. He often referred to the mind as the 'soul'.

this mind, this soul, by which I am what I am is entirely distinct from the body... even if the body did not exist, the soul would not cease to be all that it is now...

Descartes said that during life, the mind and the body communicate through a tiny gland in the centre of the brain. Many people disagreed with this, but Descartes' theory sparked off a whole new debate about the mind.

Today, many people have put the mind and body back together again. The study of the brain has become very important. Modern mind theories link the processes of the mind to the nervous system inside the body.

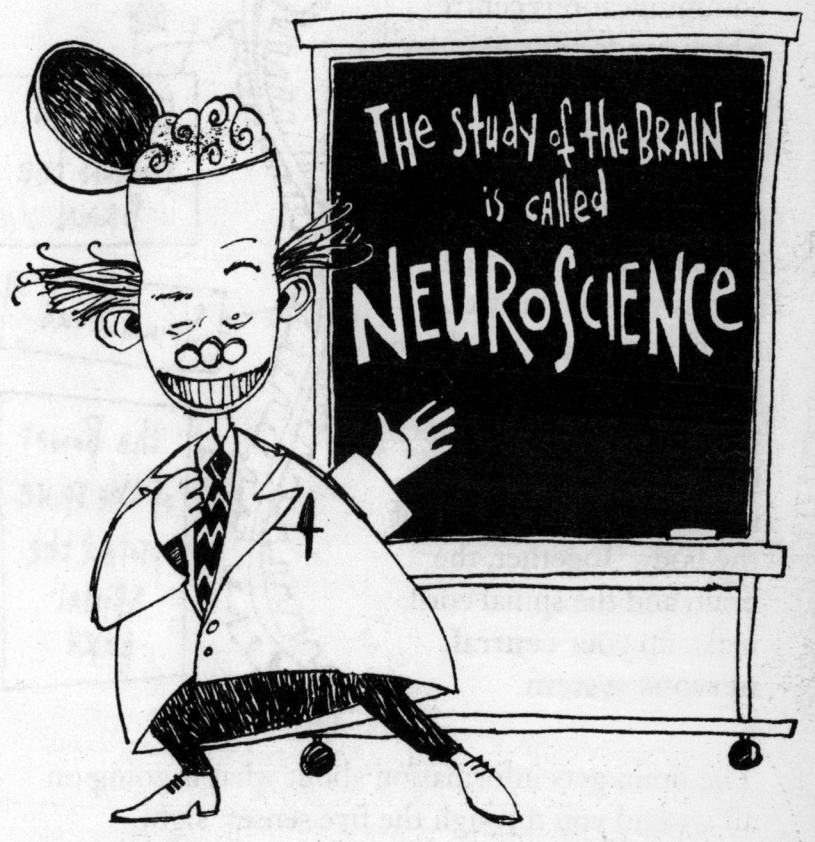

THE study of the BRAIN is called NEUROSCIENCE

So let's start our search for the mind by looking deep into the brain and beyond …

JOURNEY TO THE CENTRE OF THE BRAIN

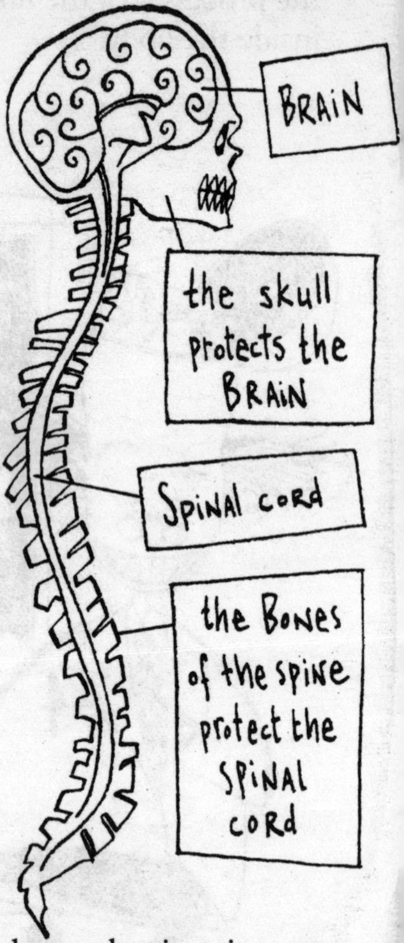

The search for the mind starts with the **brain** – the communications centre which sends out messages all over the body and receives them back. The main link between the brain and the body is the **spinal cord**, a bundle of nerves which runs from the base of the brain down through the middle of the spine. More nerves branch off the spinal cord to connect with every part of the body. Together, the brain and the spinal cord make up your **central nervous system**.

BRAIN

the skull protects the BRAIN

Spinal cord

the Bones of the spine protect the SPINAL cord

The brain gets information about what is going on all around you through the five senses: sight, hearing, taste, touch and smell.

sight HEARING taste touch smell

QUIZ

Are these amazing brain statements true or false?

1. You only ever use about 10% of the full potential of your brain.
2. People with bigger brains are more intelligent.
3. A few weeks before birth, an unborn child has more brain cells than when it's born.
4. The brain uses about 33% of the body's oxygen supply.
5. The average nerve cell in the brain is connected to about 10,000 other nerve cells.

ANSWERS

1. False: it's probably even less than this!
2. False: there's no direct link between brain size and intelligence.
3. True: thousands of nerve cells die off before birth.
4. True.
5. True: but some are connected to at least 50,000 and probably more.

So what does the brain actually look like? Underneath the skull it's a whitish-yellowish colour, folded and wrinkled like a walnut. Underneath this layer, it looks rather like a pinkish wobbly jelly …

CORTEX
folded layer about 3 mm thick that covers the cerebrum

CORPUS CALLOSUM
the bundle of nerves that joins the two hemispheres of the cerebrum

AMYGDALA
involved with memory may also control emotions

HIPPOCAMPUS
involved in memory interpreting smell and other sensory information

PONS
the part of the Brain stem that deals with messages about movement

MEDULLA
the part of the Brain stem that controls basic functions such as breathing & digestion

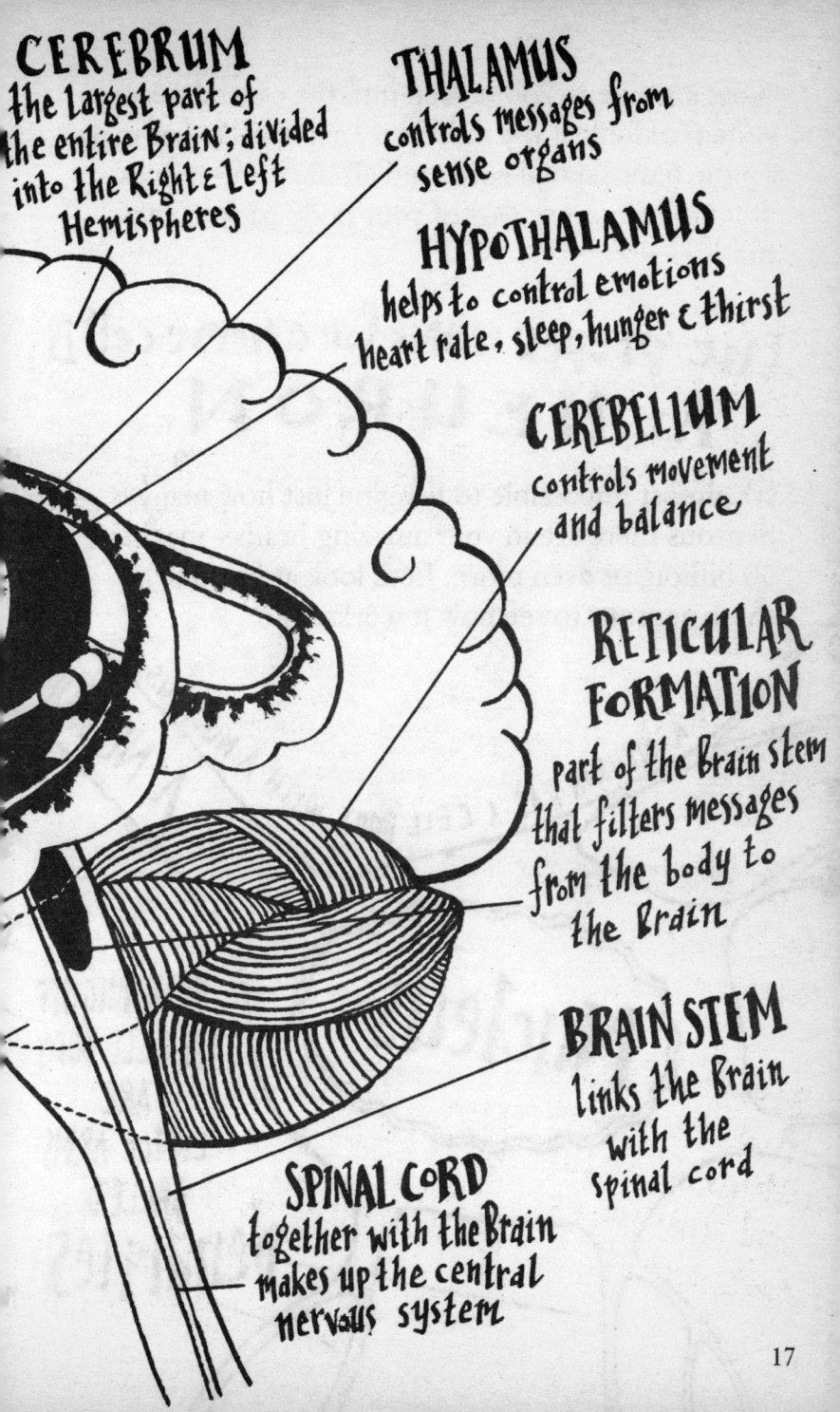

CEREBRUM
the largest part of
the entire Brain; divided
into the Right & Left
Hemispheres

THALAMUS
controls messages from
sense organs

HYPOTHALAMUS
helps to control emotions
heart rate, sleep, hunger & thirst

CEREBELLUM
controls movement
and balance

**RETICULAR
FORMATION**
part of the brain stem
that filters messages
from the body to
the Brain

BRAIN STEM
links the Brain
with the
spinal cord

SPINAL CORD
together with the Brain
makes up the central
nervous system

17

Now it's time to zoom deep into the central nervous system to look at the individual nerve cells that make up the brain, spinal cord, and all the other nerves that connect every part of your body back to the brain.

The proper name for a nerve cell is A NEURON

It's almost impossible to imagine just how many neurons there are in your amazing brain – maybe 50 billion, or even more. Let's look at just one of these neurons to see how it works.

A NEURON HAS A CELL BODY WITH A NUCLEUS

A NEURON

Nucleus

BRANCHING OFF THE CELL BODY ARE LITTLE ARMS CALLED Dendrites

As a message travels along a nerve it is transmitted from one neuron to another. Neurons pass on messages in the form of tiny bursts of electricity. Usually, an **axon** transmits the message and a **dendrite** receives it. The axon and dendrite don't actually touch – there is a minute gap between them – many times thinner than the layer of ink on this paper. The message jumps across the gap.

ALSO HAS ONE LONG ARM CALLED AN AXON

NOW THIS IS THE CLEVER PART

Each neuron in your brain is connected by its axon and dendrites to lots and lots of other neurons. In fact, scientists think that some neurons are connected to at least 50,000 others! So, if there are billions of neurons in your brain, and some are connected to at least 50,000 others, that makes … far too many connections to count!

this is the secret of the BRAIN

CONNECTIVITY

We'll look more closely at the brain's connectivity later on. Meanwhile, let's go back to the brain map and look again at the wrinkly walnut part called the **cortex**.

FACT: the cortex is deeply folded and grooved. This means that it has a much larger surface area than if it were flat, so more neurons can be squeezed in.

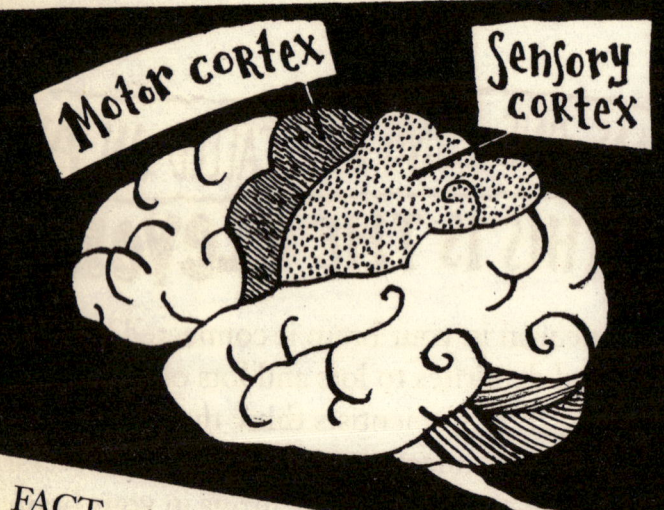

Motor cortex

Sensory cortex

FACT: scientists have discovered that different areas of your cortex have different jobs. The strip of cortex that runs across the top of your head deals with information coming in from the outside world through your senses: the **sensory cortex**. Another strip sends information out to your muscles to control movement in your body: the **motor cortex**. The area of cortex at the back of your head deals with sight.

Let's go back to *The Mind Manual for Teeth Brushing*. 'Step 1: Recognise correct brush.' That's easy, isn't it? But even the simplest actions require your brain to co-ordinate lots of different information.

Outgoing message to eye muscles: LOOK AT BRUSHES.

Incoming message from eyes: RED BRUSH RECOGNISED.

Outgoing message to muscles of hand and arm: PREPARE TO GRASP RED BRUSH.

Incoming message from touch sensors in hand: BRUSH SEIZED.

And that's only step 1!

The cortex covers the **cerebrum**, which is divided into two halves, or **hemispheres**. No one knows exactly why, but the right hemisphere controls the left side of your body, and the left hemisphere controls the right side of your body. The two halves of your brain are good at different things.

Which side of your brain are you exercising in these puzzles?

1 Which two of these figures are identical?

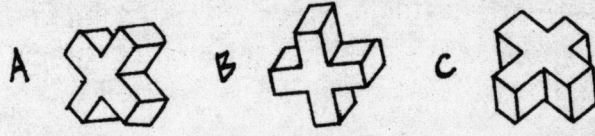

A   B   C

2 Tim has 5 cakes, Tom has 6 and Tam has 7. Tom gives 2 cakes to Tim and 3 to Tam. Tam then gives 2 cakes to Tim. How many cakes do they have now?

3 Which is the odd one out?

Of course, even though the two halves of your brain are better at different things, they don't work separately. The right and left hemispheres are joined together by a thick bundle of over 200 million nerves, called the **corpus callosum**. So you don't use just the right side of your brain to play music or just the left side of your brain to solve a mathematical puzzle. You are always using your whole brain.

Every second of every day you breathe in and out, you digest food, your heart pumps blood – all without your being aware of it at all. This is because many parts of your body run on automatic. If you had to concentrate the whole time on keeping your heart going or on breathing in and out you would never be able to think about or do anything else!

The main regions of your brain responsible for controlling all these automatic functions are the brain stem and the hypothalamus. The hypothalamus is about the size of a pea. Yet it controls your breathing, body temperature, hunger, thirst … and much more.

If there is too much carbon dioxide in your blood, the hypothalamus sends messages to other parts of your brain to make you breathe faster, so that you take in more oxygen.

If your body temperature is too cold, the hypothalamus sends messages to other parts of the brain to start you shivering. The shivering movement of your muscles helps to create heat.

If your blood is too salty, the hypothalamus sends messages to make you feel thirsty. A glass of orange squash soon puts things right.

Imagine that you are sitting in your living room. The TV is on, your sister is chatting on the phone, the clock is ticking, the dog is barking, from upstairs there is the sound of music playing on your brother's stereo system. You are trying to read your favourite book. In fact, you are so enthralled by the twists and turns of the plot that you hardly notice all the noise and action going on around you. How does your amazing brain manage to block out all the unwanted messages that are bombarding it?

One of the most important jobs that the brain does is to sift the information coming in to sort out what is important and what isn't. Every second, millions of messages are flashed to the brain through the spinal cord. These messages are filtered by the **reticular formation**, deep inside the brain stem. The reticular formation dampens down the unimportant messages (such as the sounds of the TV, your sister, the clock, the dog, your brother's music) and sends the important messages (the words in your book) on to the correct area of your brain.

If your reticular formation didn't dampen down some of the activity of your brain, you would soon have …

MESSAGE OVERLOAD!

What clues have we got so far on our search for the MIND?

CLUE: The central nervous system of the body is made up of the brain and the spinal cord. The brain is the communications centre, and the spinal cord is the main link between the brain and the rest of the body.

CLUE: Different areas of the brain have different jobs.

CLUE: The brain is made up of billions of nerve cells called neurons which transmit messages in the form of tiny bursts of electricity.

So is the mind inside the brain? Or is it inside the whole of the central nervous system? We've found out a little about how the brain actually works, but there are still lots of questions to be answered!

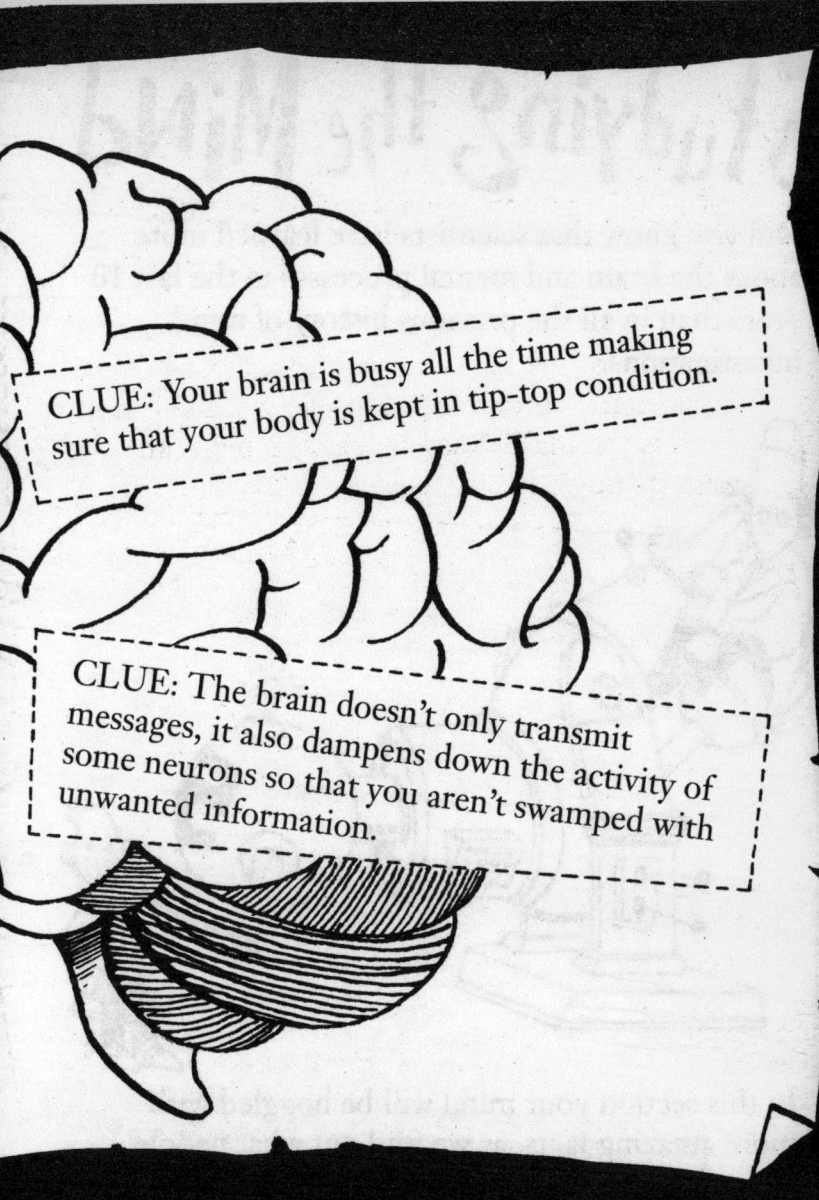

CLUE: Your brain is busy all the time making sure that your body is kept in tip-top condition.

CLUE: The brain doesn't only transmit messages, it also dampens down the activity of some neurons so that you aren't swamped with unwanted information.

For instance, how do we remember things? What happens to our minds when we go to sleep? Why do we cry when we're sad? Do animals have minds? If you want to find out, just read on …

Studying the Mind

Did you know that scientists have learned more about the brain and mental processes in the last 10 years than in all the previous history of mind investigations?

In this section your mind will be boggled with more amazing facts, as we find out what people thought about the mind in the past, and look at the latest, most shiny, most up-to-date, laser-powered, turbo-charged, mind-blowing machines used to study the mind today.

Prehistoric human skulls with holes cut or drilled into the side have been found in many parts of the world, but particularly in ancient burial sites in Peru, South America. (Making a hole in the skull is called **trepanation**.) No one knows for certain why these holes were cut. Perhaps they were an ancient cure for headaches!

One method people used to try to find out about the brain was to cut up dead bodies. (This process is called **dissection**.) But many people disapproved of this, so dissections often had to be carried out in great secrecy. The famous artist, Leonardo da Vinci (1472-1519) secretly dissected over 300 human bodies and made more than 1500 detailed drawings of his findings. On the other hand, the great physician Andreas Vesalius (1514-64) performed some of his human dissections before audiences of more than 500 students and doctors!

The Strange History of Franz Joseph Gall (1758–1828)

Part I
A school in Baden, Germany, 1767.
The young Franz Gall is pleased because he got an A+ for his essay and his friend only got a B (tee hee!). However, Franz is less pleased that his friend always beats him in spelling tests; his friend's memory seems to be much better than Franz's. Then Franz notices something strange ... his friend has rather bulging eyes. So do several other people in the class, all of whom do better than Franz in spelling tests ...

What can this mean?

Part II
A lecture theatre in Vienna, Austria, 1796.
The grown-up Franz Gall - now a doctor - is lecturing on his new theory of brain localization.

The fact that people with good memories often have bulging eyes is caused by the unusually developed shape of the brain area behind the eyes. Similarly, people who are good speakers have a lump in the skull towards the front of the head. By examining hundreds of skulls I have discovered areas relating to 27 different characteristics, including 'destructiveness', 'mirthfulness' and 'acquisitiveness'. I call this new science of the brain, 'phrenology'.

Gall's theory was quickly proved wrong, but it sparked off investigations into the theory that different parts of the brain have different jobs … which of course is true! (And he became a very rich man.)

Learning by Accident

Throughout history, scientists have learned about the workings of the mind by studying people with damaged brains. One of the most famous cases was that of Phineas Gage.

Phineas Gage was a hard-working, happy-go-lucky man who worked on the railways in New England, USA.

In 1848 Gage had a terrible accident. An explosion sent a metal rod more than a metre long straight through his head. The rod went in through Gage's left cheek and came out through the top of his skull. The rod was found, covered in bits of brain, several metres away.

Gage was very ill for the next few weeks, but after a month it seemed that he would survive. But something very strange had occurred …

Gage was no longer the same person. He swore and was bad-tempered, he was no longer dependable and he lost his job on the railways. So what had happened?

Several scientists took interest in Gage's transformation. Could it be that Gage's character had changed because the front part of his brain had been blown away?

Today, we know that the front part of the brain plays a part in emotions and expression, so this probably accounts for the reason why Gage was no longer Gage!

In the 1980s, safe methods of taking pictures of the living brain became widely available, and this amazing technology provided scientists with huge amounts of new information. There are three main ways to take pictures of the brain.

1   X-ray computed tomography (CT)
This makes a computer picture of a slice of the brain by measuring the density of the brain tissue.

2   Nuclear magnetic resonance (NMR)
NMR makes an even more detailed picture of the brain 'slice' than CT.

3   Positron-emission tomography (PET)
This can be used to highlight which areas of the brain are most active at certain times.

Another method of studying the brain is **electroencephalography** – or, if you can't get your mind around those 22 letters, **EEG** for short. EEG is a way of measuring the tiny electrical messages that are whizzing around your brain the whole time. These electrical signals are shown on a screen or a paper chart as wavy lines. EEG is often used in the study of sleep.

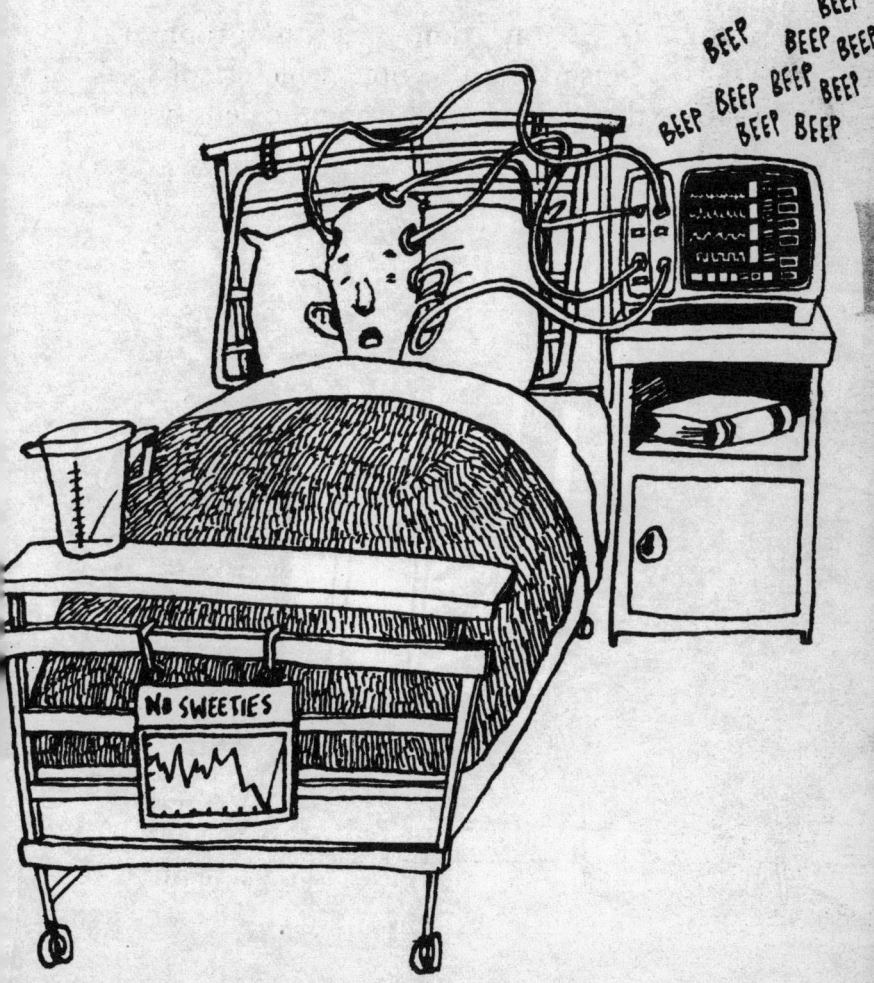

One of the main uses for modern brain-scanning equipment is to identify and try to cure brain disorders. In the past, people suffering from mental illnesses were thought to be possessed by demon spirits. They were usually locked up and treated with terrible cruelty because people didn't understand what was wrong with them and were often afraid of them.

Today, doctors and scientists are discovering that many so-called 'mental' illnesses are actually caused by physical disorders in the brain.

Schizophrenia is the name given to an illness that has many different symptoms. People suffering from schizophrenia hear voices, behave in odd ways that they cannot explain, jumble up their words and thoughts. Doctors do not yet fully understand what causes schizophrenia, but they think it has something to do with abnormalities in the structure and the chemistry of the brain.

Alzheimers disease also attacks the brain. The neurons in the cortex and hippocampus areas of the brain shrivel and die. People with Alzheimers lose their memory and their ability to communicate. Doctors do not know what causes this disease, or why it is more likely to attack older people.

Some illnesses have their origins deep within the mind, such fears of objects or situations. These fears are called **phobias**.

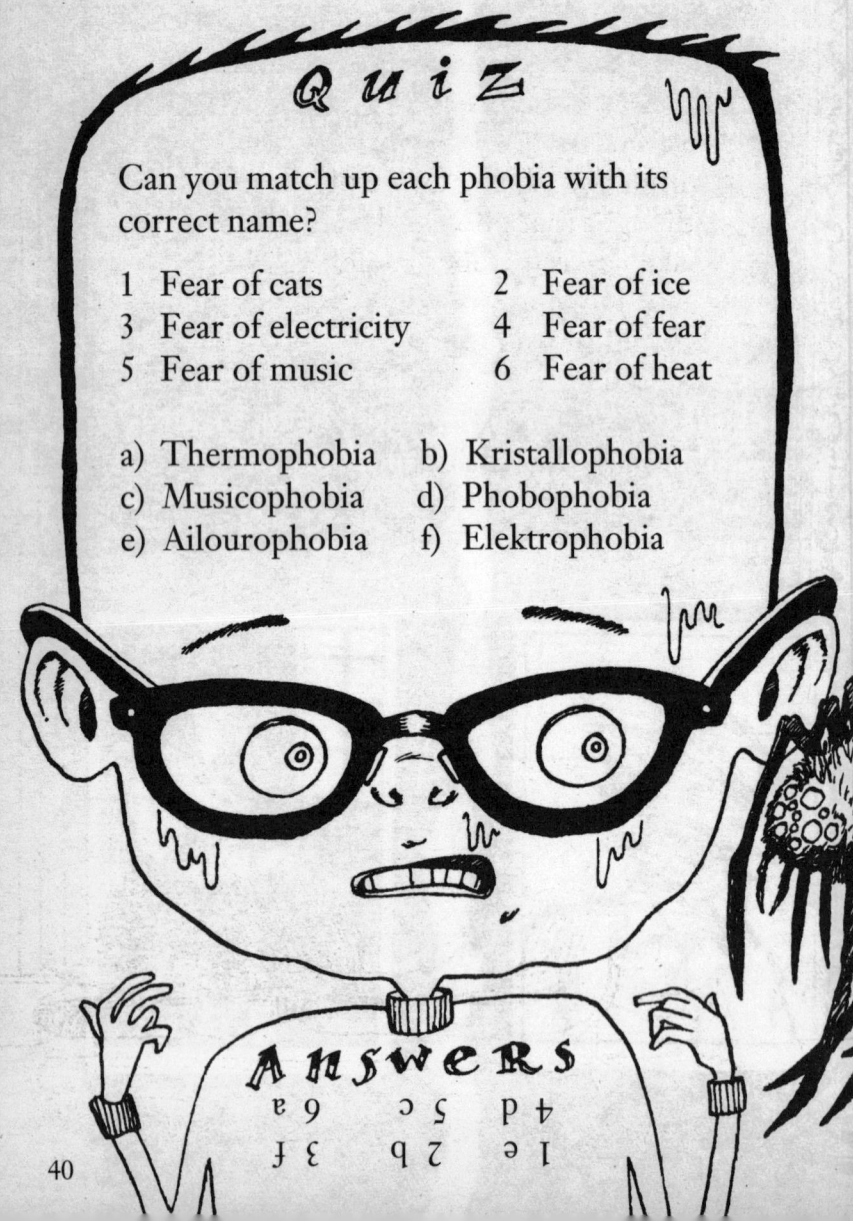

Q u i z

Can you match up each phobia with its correct name?

1 Fear of cats
2 Fear of ice
3 Fear of electricity
4 Fear of fear
5 Fear of music
6 Fear of heat

a) Thermophobia
b) Kristallophobia
c) Musicophobia
d) Phobophobia
e) Ailourophobia
f) Elektrophobia

Answers

1e 2b 3f 4d 5c 6a

Sigmund Freud (1856-1939) was very interested in phobias. He thought that they were the outward signs of a much deeper fear buried in the mind.

Freud said that there is the **conscious** part of the mind – the bit we use all the time to think, to make decisions, to speak. Then there is the **unconscious** part, which works away all the time without you being aware of it.

It is thought that phobias develop because they make you remember an unpleasant experience in your past. You may not remember this experience consciously, but it's still there in your unconscious. For instance, someone who is afraid of small, enclosed spaces such as lifts (a fear called **claustrophobia**) may have had a frightening experience being stuck in a small, enclosed space as a child. They have forgotten the experience, but it has remained in their unconscious, resurfacing every time they walk into a lift.

Dr Franz Anton Mesmer (1734-1815) was all the rage in Vienna in the 1770s. His method of treating patients was to point a large magnet at his patients. The power of the magnet was supposed to cause a trance-like state, from which the patient would eventually emerge 'cured' from whatever illness had affected them. But **mesmerism**, as his technique came to be called, was denounced by the Viennese doctors and Dr Mesmer was forced to flee to Paris, where he set up another successful practice!

Several people continued to practise mesmerism in the 19th century, although they did away with the magnet! A French doctor found that he could put patients into a trance-like state by staring into their eyes and telling them that they felt sleepy. If he then suggested to patients that their illness was cured, the symptoms often disappeared. Similarly, an English doctor cut off the leg of a patient who was put into a trance by mesmerism. The patient was reported to feel no pain.

SO I GO IN AND THIS CHAP SHOWS ME HIS WATCH. NEXT THING I KNOW IT'S NO MORE FOOTBALL.

Mesmerism was renamed **hypnosis** (from the Greek word 'hypnos', meaning 'sleep').

What is happening in hypnosis?

When someone is in a hypnotic trance they have no control over their words or behaviour on a conscious level, but the hypnotist is able to suggest ideas to their unconscious mind. The easiest way to try to understand hypnosis is to look at some more of the amazing things that can happen during a hypnotic trance.

The woman's skin comes up in blisters where the pencil has touched. Her unconscious mind has accepted the suggestion that the pencil was red-hot, and has sent messages to her body to react appropriately.

Sometimes, hypnosis is used to find hidden memories.

Imagine you are standing on a street corner one day when suddenly you see two men running out of the local bank. They've got stockings pulled down over their heads … they're brandishing guns … it's a hold-up! And now they're jumping into the getaway car and roaring off down the street … Quick! Get the registration number! But it's too late – you saw the number and you've forgotten it already.

But the number IS still there – in your unconscious. Under hypnosis, the hypnotist may be able to make you 'find' the number once more – dragging it out of your unconscious mind.

The study of the mind is called **psychology** (pronounced si-ko-lo-jee). This science attempts to understand the human mind and human behaviour.

As we have seen, phobias, depression, schizophrenia, Alzheimer's disease and many more are all problems or illnesses of the mind, some of which are caused by physical changes in the brain. Sometimes, these can be treated with drugs which help to restore the correct balance of chemicals in the brain.

Other illnesses and problems are connected to the unconscious workings of the mind itself. There are hundreds of different methods of treating these – far too many to tell you about in this short tour of psychology. But you may have heard of **psychiatry** (pronounced si-ki-a-tree), which is concerned with the care and treatment of people with illnesses of the mind and **psychotherapy** (pronounced ski-ko-ther-a-pee), which is concerned with the treatment of emotional problems in the mind.

Thanks for the Memory

How important is memory? To answer this question, try imagining life without memory. You would have to learn even the most basic actions every day.

You wouldn't remember from day to day who your friends or even family were.

In fact you wouldn't even remember the words to ask who people were or how to do something.

So memory is absolutely crucial to learning, speaking, doing – in fact, living!

So how does memory work?

Look at this group of letters for about 15 seconds.

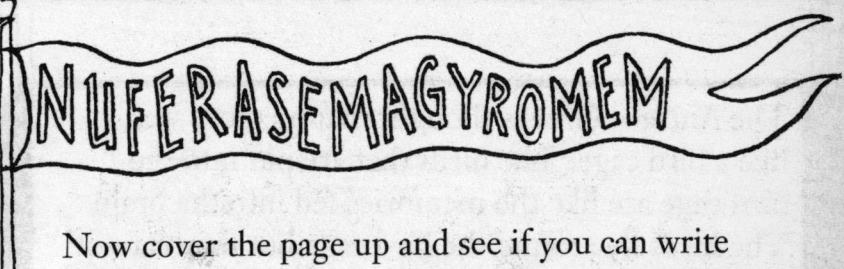

NUFERASEMAGYROMEM

Now cover the page up and see if you can write the letters down in the right order.

How many did you get right? What stages did your mind go through to memorise the letters?

1 The information is fed into your brain.
2 The information is stored in the brain.
3 The information is retrieved when you need to use it again.

These three stages are often called:

1 **encoding**, 2 **storage**, 3 **retrieval**.

The Ancient Greeks thought that memory was like a bird cage! The birds that are put into the bird cage are like the memories fed into the brain. The birds fly around the bird cage but they cannot escape – like the memories inside the brain. When you want to get hold of a particular bird you must reach into the cage and trap it – just like trying to retrieve a memory.

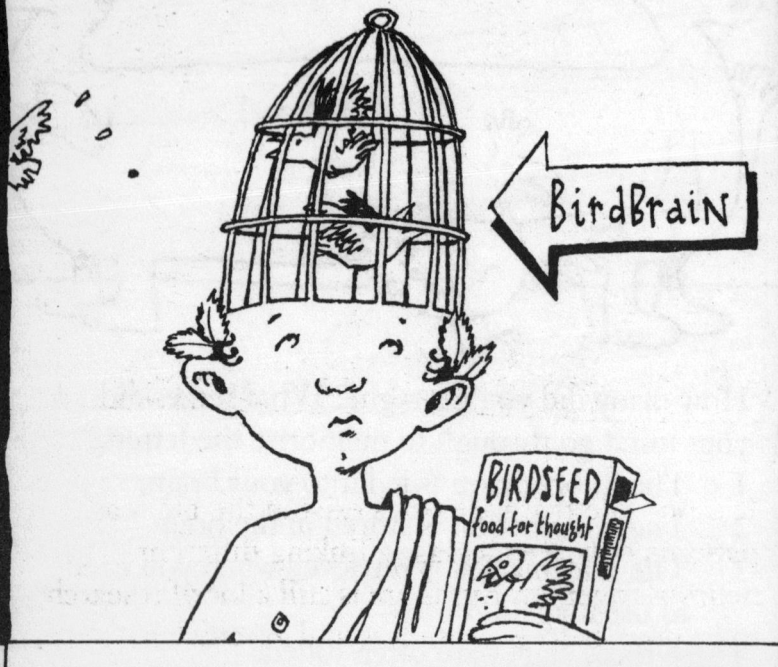

Of course, memories don't fly around the brain like birds! Scientists have learned about which bits of the brain are concerned with memory by studying people who have lost their memory because of an accident. The scientists found that these people often had damage to the hippocampus and the amygdala regions of their brains.

It is possible that memories exist in the brain as patterns of nerve messages, linking different neurons together. But there is still a lot of research to be done before we understand exactly how memory works inside the brain.

It seems very likely that there are several different kinds of memory inside your brain. Think about what happens when you look up a friend's telephone number.

Five minutes later you suddenly need to ring Egbert again. Can you remember the number? Probably not. This is an example of the use of your **short-term memory**. In your short-term memory, information is held for as long as it is needed, then discarded.

You also have a **long-term memory**. This is where you keep all the information you need for living, such as how to recognise people, use language, play your trumpet, read your book. This is also where you keep memories of events from long ago – such as building a huge sandcastle on the beach when you were small! You can even remember tastes (such as your first ice cream) and smells (for instance, seaweed), also sounds (like the cries of seagulls) and feelings (for example, the disappointment of the tide coming in and washing your sandcastle away!)

Long-term memories stay in your brain. Even if you don't ride your bike for a while or play on your computer, you don't forget how to use them. You may be a bit rusty to start with, but the memories soon come flooding back.

TEST YOUR VISUAL MEMORY
Look at these designs for about 15 seconds.
Now turn the page.

TEST YOUR VISUAL MEMORY

How many of these designs are the same as the ones you've just looked at on the previous page?

How many of the designs did you get right? Most people find visual information easier to remember than words or numbers. Think back to the letters you saw on page 49. Can you remember them? Would you find it easier if you knew they spelt out the words, MEMORY GAMES ARE FUN, backwards? As soon as the letters are organised into chunks of information they are much easier to remember.

Try to memorise this square of letters:

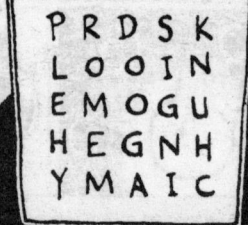

It's not so easy, is it? Now start at the bottom right-hand corner and read each row vertically from bottom to top. 'Chunking' is the method of grouping information together to make it easier to remember. Most people find it difficult to remember lists of numbers, words, or letters with more than 7 items.

try remembering these lines of numbers

396
2685
71396
472395
6398142
59352815
274958351

Although most people can remember lists of only 7 things, there are ways of improving your memory. One of the best ways is to use **mnemonics.** Mnemonics work by association. For instance, imagine you want to remember two completely separate things:

The best way to remember both things is to link them together, forming an image in your mind. The more ridiculous the image, the more likely you are to remember both things!

Here's a very well-known mnemonic. Do you know what it helps you to remember?

Richard Of York Gained Battles In Vain

Answer: the colours of the rainbow – red, orange, yellow, green, blue, indigo and violet.

Some people have photographic memories. They can look at the page of a book and after only a few seconds they can remember that page exactly. They actually 'see' an image of the page before them, suggesting that they have a very developed visual memory.

This is my pal Polly Roid

(poor joke)

How many times do you forget a word or a name that you know you know? Why do we forget things?

If there's a failure in any one of the three processes of memory - encoding, storage and retrieval - then this can lead to forgetting. Sometimes you didn't store the information in the first place. Sometimes the memory is in your brain (encoded and stored) but you cannot retrieve it. You need some kind of clue or memory jog to retrieve that particular memory.

Sometimes new information takes over from old, out-of-date information. If you move house, how quickly do you forget your old telephone number and remember the new one?

Freud had an interesting theory about memory and forgetting. He said that some experiences are so painful that the mind deliberately 'forgets' them. These experiences are stored in the unconscious part of the mind. This kind of forgetting is called **repression**.

Some accidents and diseases cause people to forget. A blow to the head may damage the parts of the brain concerned with memory. A stroke stops the flow of blood to the head, and kills neurons in the brain. This can also affect memory.

Your body is constantly taking in information about the world around you. Let's look more closely at your five senses and what is actually happening in the mind as it processes all this information.

The first surprise is that there aren't just five senses, there are six! Hearing, sight, smell, taste, touch … and a sense of balance that lets you know the position of your limbs. Think about it! You don't have to look at your feet to know where they are! This sixth sense allows you to find your mouth with a forkful of food, and stops you poking out your eye when you scratch your nose.

Hearing: your ears are the very outermost parts of your hearing system. Most of the working parts for hearing are deep within your head.

 **Smell**: sensors at the back of your nose respond to smells - but on the whole, humans aren't as good at smelling as many animals.

Taste: different areas of your tongue have different sensors which respond to sweetness, sourness and saltiness.

Touch: you have touch sensors all over your body, but the most sensitive areas to touch are your fingers and your mouth. Your touch sensors respond to pressure and to heat and cold. Life without touch would be very difficult and dangerous. For instance, you wouldn't know when you put your hand on something hot, or your foot on something sharp, or if a wasp had just stung you …

Find out more about **sight** over the page …

Pupil

The black circle in the centre of your eye. Changes size to allow more or less light into the eye.

Optic nerve

Information from the light-sensitive cells in the retina is taken along the optic nerve to the brain.

Blind spot

A tiny area on the retina where the optic nerve leaves the eye. There are no sensor cells in this area, so it is literally a 'blind' spot!

Visual cortex

Information received through the eye is processed in an area of the cortex at the back of the brain.

People often say that the eye works rather like a camera: light enters the camera through the lens; the lens focuses the light; the light forms an image on the film at the back of the camera. Also, the film in a camera is sensitive to light, like the cells of the retina.

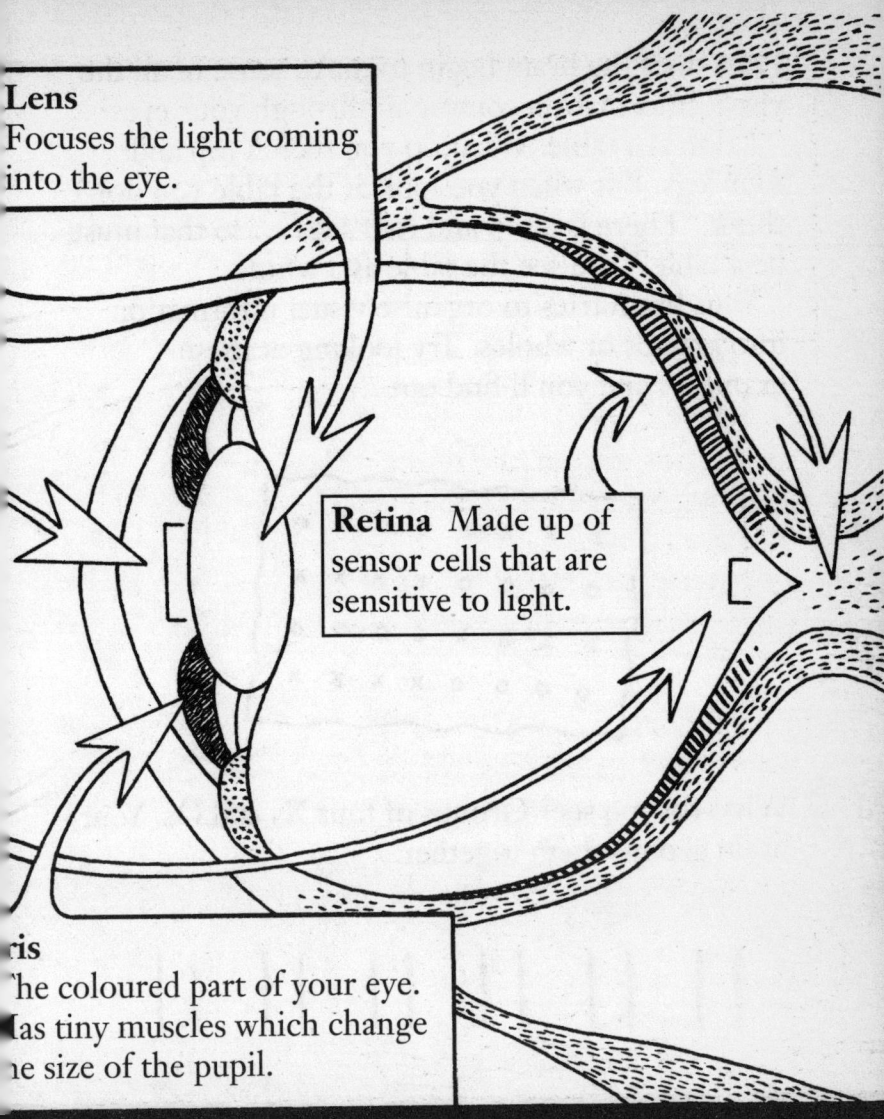

Lens
Focuses the light coming
into the eye.

Retina Made up of
sensor cells that are
sensitive to light.

Iris
The coloured part of your eye.
Has tiny muscles which change
the size of the pupil.

But while a camera can only take one picture at a
time, the retina is continually collecting
information which is sent through the optic nerve
to the brain. In your sensory cortex at the back of
your head, your amazing brain interprets all this
information.

63

How does the brain begin to make sense of all the visual information coming in through your eyes?

Look at a table. What do you see? A top and four legs. But when you look at the table you don't think, 'There is a top and four legs … so that must be a table!' You see the table as a whole.

Your brain tries to organise visual information into groups or wholes. Try looking at these examples and you'll find out …

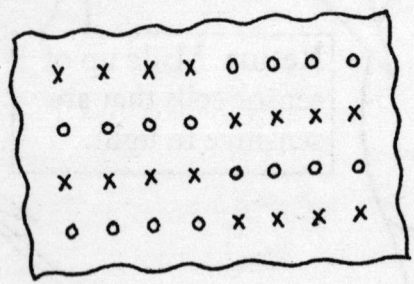

What do you see? Groups of four Xs and Os. Your brain groups them together.

What do you see? Pairs of lines separated by spaces. Try seeing the lines as groups of line-space-line. It's almost impossible because your brain groups the lines that are close together.

What do you see? Two curving lines of dots. Your brain groups the dots together to make the lines.

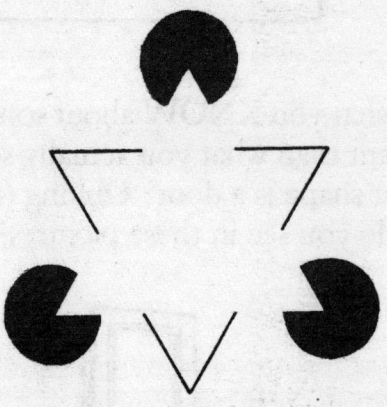

What do you see? Even though none of the shapes is complete, your brain completes each shape and interprets it.

You see a triangle, but it's not there!

Sometimes your brain is confused by the information being received through your eyes. For example, what do you see in this picture? A vase or two faces? Your brain can interpret this picture in two ways.

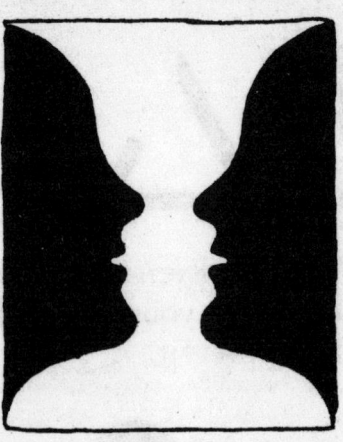

Sometimes, what you KNOW about something is more important than what you actually see. For instance, what shape is a door? Oblong (usually!). What shape do you see in these pictures?

The door in these pictures is actually three quite different shapes - and only one of them is an oblong! But your brain knows that a door is always an oblong, and this is how it interprets the pictures.

Your brain is very clever at recognizing patterns. What do all these different shapes have in common?

How does your amazing brain know that they are all the same letter? Maybe it stores patterns and compares them against the new information that is coming in all the time... No one understands completely how it does this.

Sometimes what you see fools or confuses your brain. Try these puzzles:

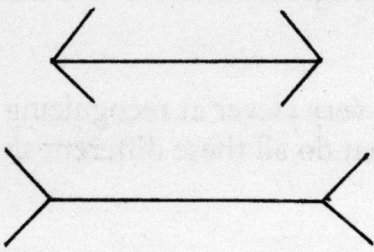

Which line is longer? In fact, they are the same! Your eye is fooled by the arrows on the end.

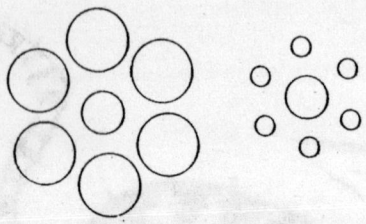

Which of the central circles is bigger? Again, they are the same! This time your eye is fooled by the context - the large circles make the middle circle look small, the small circles make the middle circle look large.

These Puzzles are called

One of the best-known optical illusions happens every time you go to the cinema. At the cinema you see a moving picture, don't you?

In fact, a cinema film is made up of thousands and thousands of still pictures. These still pictures are flashed on to the cinema screen at the rate of 24 per second. Your brain interprets them as one continuous moving picture. So now you know that you shouldn't necessarily believe what you see!

Learning & Intelligence

You may think that learning is something you only do at school …

… but in fact you are learning all the time. There are many different kinds of learning.

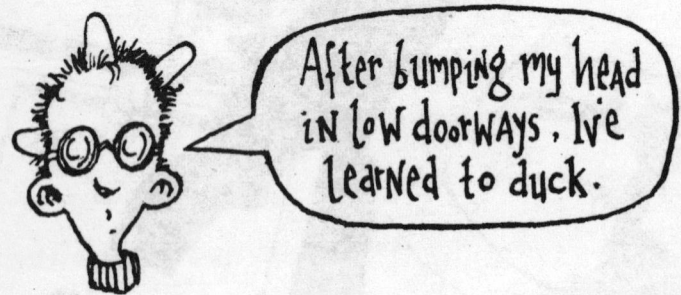

After bumping my head in low doorways, I've learned to duck.

Learning can mean forming a habit.

Go AWAY AND LEARN this properly!

HIGHWAY CODE

Learning can mean memorising something so that you know it off by heart.

Learning can mean becoming skilled at something.

Learning can mean finding out or discovering something.

But all these different kinds of learning involve experience and memory. You are continually learning by experience. If something gives you pleasure (such as chocolate toffee ice cream - yum!), you will remember the experience and want to repeat it (more please!). But if something causes you pain (too much chocolate toffee ice cream = bad stomach ache), you will remember the warning signals caused by the pain and try not to repeat that experience (I must remember not to have five helpings of chocolate toffee ice cream).

But what is actually happening inside your brain to allow you to learn? To find out, we must dive back into the microscopic world of neurons.

Here's what happens when a baby grows inside its mother's womb for nine months ...

After only 19 days, the formation of the brain begins ...

Between eight and 13 weeks, there is a huge growth spurt in the brain when millions of neurons are formed ...

About 10 weeks before birth, there is another spurt as neurons make millions of connections ...

This spurt continues for about two years after birth as the brain forms huge numbers of complicated neuron networks ...

As we found out earlier, connectivity is the secret of the brain. The number of neurons in the brain is not as important as the number of connections made between the neurons in the brain. You can see how quickly a baby learns by the difference in the number of neuron connections at birth and three months later ...

AMAZING BABY FACTS

1 A baby learns to recognize its mother's voice while it is still inside the womb. At birth, it prefers its mother's voice to other sounds.
2 At birth, the senses are well-developed, for example, a normal baby watches moving objects with its eyes and turns towards an unusual noise.
3 Within a few days a new-born baby has already learned to recognize the faces of its mother and father.
4 Even very young babies imitate the expressions on peoples' faces - smiling, frowning, opening the mouth wide, sticking out the tongue ...

The learning process continues at top speed for the first few years of life. Think about all the things you learned to do between the ages of 0 and 5!

One of the most important studies of how children learn was made by a French psychologist Jean Piaget (1896-1980). He said that children learn through their experiences of the world around them. As they learn, their minds become capable of more complicated ways of thinking.

One of Piaget's experiments shows the difference between the ways of thinking of a four-year-old and a seven-year-old. Piaget took three glasses - two were small and fat, and one was tall and thin. He put the same amount of water into each of the small, fat glasses.

Then he poured the water from one of the small, fat glasses into the tall, thin glass.

The four-year-old cannot recognize that the quantity of water stays the same, even though it looks different. But by seven years old, a child has learned to understand that it is the shape that has changed, not the quantity.

Without memory, you would not be able to learn. Without language, you would not be able to communicate.

Descartes, lying in bed and thinking hard, wrote that 'language belongs to man alone ...'. Animals have many methods of communicating with each other, but only humans use words - speech and writing - to communicate.

Some scientists have done experiments to try to teach chimpanzees to talk human language. But although chimps can learn words and phrases, they cannot learn grammar. Grammar is the way words are organised to make them understandable. Without grammar it wouldn't matter how many words you know - no one would understand what you were on about!

Insert some English grammar, and you get:

Children start to learn the rules of grammar at a very early age. But they learn the rules from experience. For example, a child that knows that more than one toy is 'toys', and more than one sweet is 'sweets', will probably call more than one sheep 'sheeps', and more than one deer 'deers'. They also have to learn that there are exceptions to rules.

After learning to speak words, the next step is to learn how to write and read words. Reading isn't just looking at words on a page ... It's recognising words, understanding their meaning and storing the information contained in the words in your amazing brain.

Have you ever thought about how you read? Simple, isn't it? You follow the words on a page from left to right, top to bottom (unless you're Chinese or Arabian). But studies have shown that when you read, your eye doesn't move steadily along a line of print. Try watching a friend's eyes as they read a book and see what happens.

Most readers move along a line of print in small jumps, taking in a few words at a time. The eye frequently checks back to words already read. It also checks forwards to tell the brain where to go next …

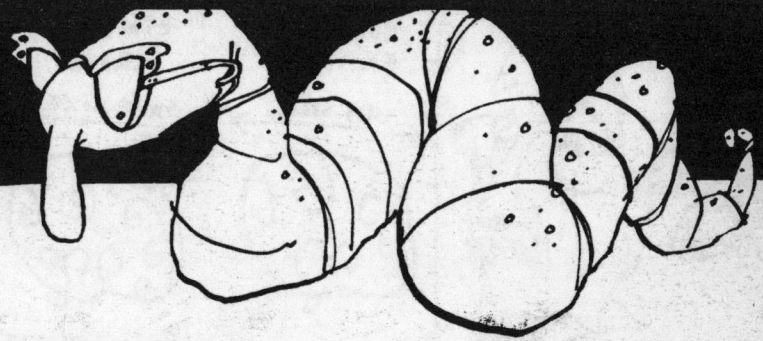

Another amazing thing about reading is how little information you actually need to understand what is being said.

Imagine a book with some of the ⸱ missing, or wi-h eve-y fif-h let-er mi-sing, r wth th vwls mssng, or with th~~e dy peppred dt pb upsdded dp auj~~ or even with bits of the print missing.

You would still be able to understand, although it would probably take some time to get used to reading it.

The size of Albert Einstein's brain was no bigger than anyone else's, yet Einstein (1879-1955) was one of the greatest geniuses who ever lived.

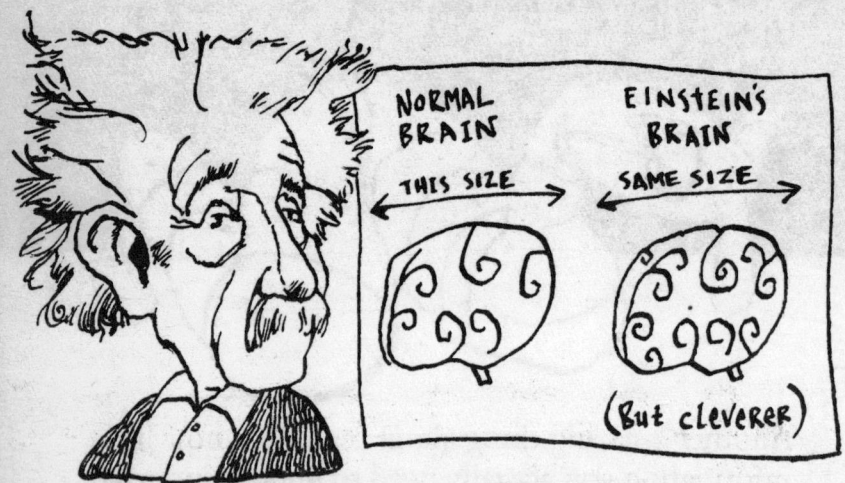

Are you a genius or a dunce? Most people are somewhere between the two extremes ... But what happens during the process of learning to make some people more intelligent than others? This is a question which has vexed people for centuries.

Let's look at what we do know.

We know that the process of learning activates more and more neuron connections in the brain.

We also know that the time just before and after birth is very important for neuron connectivity.

But does this mean that the more neuron connections that are made in your brain, the more intelligent you are?

There is some evidence to show that this is the case. Babies that have been well-fed and well looked after tend to have good mental development.
Babies that have not been given enough food - especially in the first two years of life - and whose parents have been unable to care for them well, tend to show slower mental development and lower intelligence.

But that still leaves the question, what exactly IS intelligence?

Let's look at some VERY intelligent people - the GENIUSES of the world. Which of the following would you class as geniuses?

JULIUS CAESAR
(Roman General)

LEONARDO DA VINCI
(Great Artist and helicopter inventor)

NICOLAUS COPERNICUS
founder of
(Modern Astronomy.)

WILLIAM SHAKESPEARE
(Most famous English playwright)

RENÉ DESCARTES
"I think
(therefore I am."

WOLFGANG AMADEUS MOZART
(one of the most famous composers of all time.)

MARIE CURIE
(Ground breaking research into Radioactivity)

ALBERT EINSTEIN
Devised formula
$E = MC^2$

Prof. STEPHEN HAWKING
Author of
("A Brief History of Time")

You've probably got lots of other ideas. Try making your own Genius List! But what makes a genius a genius? See how much you can find out about your geniuses and if they have anything in common. Here are some ideas to start with:

 Genius is 1% inspiration and 99% perspiration! (Said by another genius, Thomas Edison)

 Geniuses are very highly motivated. They are prepared to work hard and they have a very strong drive to succeed.

 Geniuses are open to new experiences and are not prepared to accept the 'obvious' answer. They are always 'searching'...

 Geniuses are not afraid to risk failure, and they are also prepared to learn from their mistakes.

 And finally, another genius quotation – 'The principle mark of a genius is not perfection but originality!' (Arthur Koestler)

During the 20th century, people have become very interested in trying to measure intelligence. The traditional way of doing this is by IQ (intelligence quotient) scores.

A genius has a score of around 145.
The highest IQ ever scored was 228!
To join MENSA (the society for brainy people) you need a score of about 132.
Most people score around 90 to 110 ...

But what do IQ scores actually tell us about people?
Some scientists say:

NOT VERY MUCH

SOME SCIENTISTS

Professor Howard Gardner has argued that there
isn't just one kind of intelligence, but at least seven!

Verbal (dealing with words)

Logical / Mathematical

Spatial / visual

Body intelligence

Musical / creative

Understanding of others

Self-knowledge / understanding yourself

... and there may be others! All these intelligences
are important, and different people will have
different strengths and weaknesses.

Where do you think your talents lie? Are you
stronger in one intelligence than another?
How could you improve your weaknesses?

What makes you 'You'?

Can you match the picture to the emotion:
happiness, sadness, anger, fear, surprise, disgust?

Scientists have done experiments to try to find out
whether the facial expressions that go with these
six basic emotions are recognised all over the
world. Maybe someone living in Australia would
have a different facial expression for 'fear' than
someone living in China?

The scientists showed pictures of the six emotions to people in many different countries. The answer was that most people recognised all the emotions correctly.

It seems that emotions and reactions to emotion are somehow 'wired' into the human brain. The areas of your brain that probably process emotions are the hypothalamus and the amygdala. But, of course, these areas are connected to the other bits of the brain to form a huge emotion 'network'.

Feelings aren't just in the mind – emotions cause reactions in your body. When you're sad, you cry. As you cry, your brain releases a chemical which helps you to feel better. So have a cry every now and then – it's good for you!

Crying may be good for you, but of course you don't cry every time you feel unhappy. As a baby you cried if you were hungry, or in pain, or too hot or cold … But as you grew up, you learned to control this reaction in your body. Think of a group of friends - you've probably never seen some of them cry at all … and others may cry at the slightest thing!

What would you say the difference was between the cryers and the non-cryers? Are the cryers more nervous and anxious?

Are the non-cryers more easy-going and even-tempered?

We use words like anxious, nervous, easy-going, even-tempered to try to describe someone's personality. **Personality** is the way a person is and behaves …

How do you measure someone's personality? Scientists have tried lots of different ways including interviews, looking at diaries, letters, questionaires, etc. One of the most ingenious attempts to measure personality was made by a psychologist called Hermann Rorschach. He showed people a collection of 10 inkblots and then asked them what they could 'see' in the blots.

Rorschach interpreted people's personalities by what they 'saw' in the blots. For instance, if a person saw a picture in a whole blot, Rorschach concluded that they were the type of person who would have abstract thoughts and ideas. On the other hand, if a person saw a picture in part of a blot, he concluded that they were the type of person who liked to think about real objects and happenings, and concern themselves with the details of things.

Can you assess your own personality?

Here are some personality characteristics. How many apply to you? How many apply to your friends?

the Mind asleep

Did you know that you spend up to one-third of your life asleep? But what is happening in your brain while you are asleep?

I love the nightlife.

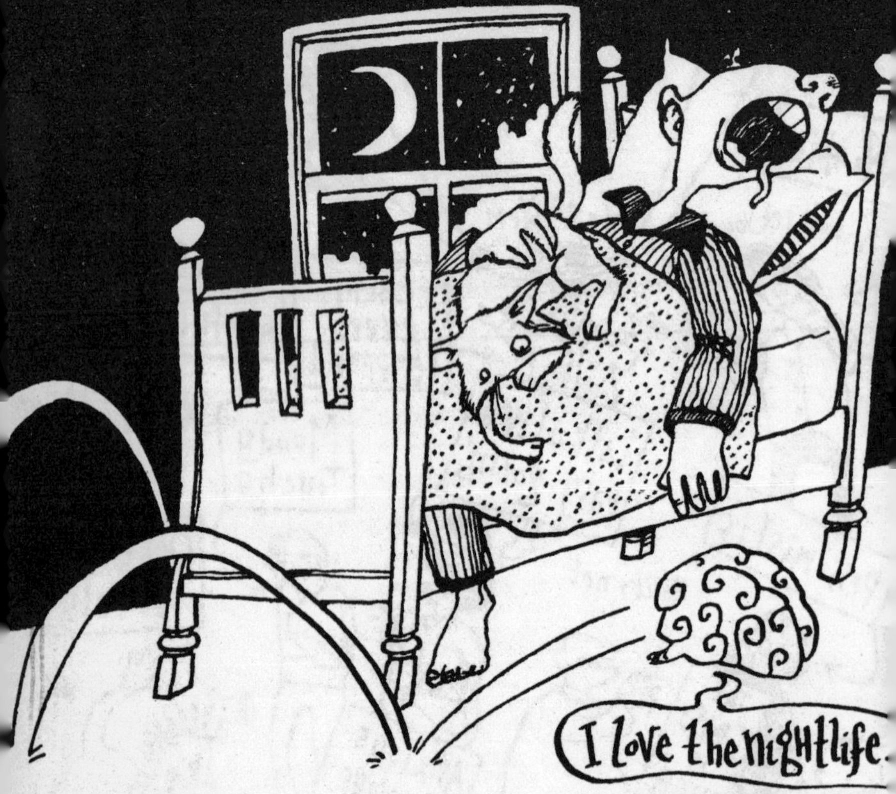

Scientists who have studied sleep have found that while your body rests during sleep, your brain is very busy. To find out what happens in your brain while you are asleep, scientists use EEGs. They have found that there are several stages in sleep.

1   Your heartbeat slows down, but at this stage
     a quiet noise could still wake you.

2   You enter deeper sleep. Beneath your eyelids
     your eyes roll slowly from side to side.

3   You are now in deep sleep. Only a very loud
     noise would wake you. You may sleep-talk
     or sleep walk.

4   You return to less deep sleep and dream. Beneath your
     eyelids your eyes flicker to and fro very quickly. This
     stage is called **rapid eye movement (REM) sleep**.

This pattern is repeated throughout the time you are asleep.

Do you remember the story of Joseph and his many-coloured coat?

When Joseph is thrown into prison in Egypt, he is in despair. But the Pharoah has an odd dream about seven hungry, thin cows which eat seven fat cows.

The Pharoah calls Joseph to interpret the dream, and Joseph says that there will be seven years of good harvests followed by seven years of famine.

This is exactly what happens!

Many Ancient peoples believed that dreams were prophecies of things to come.

Freud became interested in dreams because he believed that they could provide a route into the unconscious mind. He thought that the images and actions from a dream symbolized deeper thoughts and wishes in the unconscious part of the patient's mind ...

Today, there are two main theories of dreams:

1   That dreaming allows the brain to go over events of the day, storing information and solving difficult problems.

2   That dreaming happens so that you can forget - so that your mind can get rid of unwanted information.

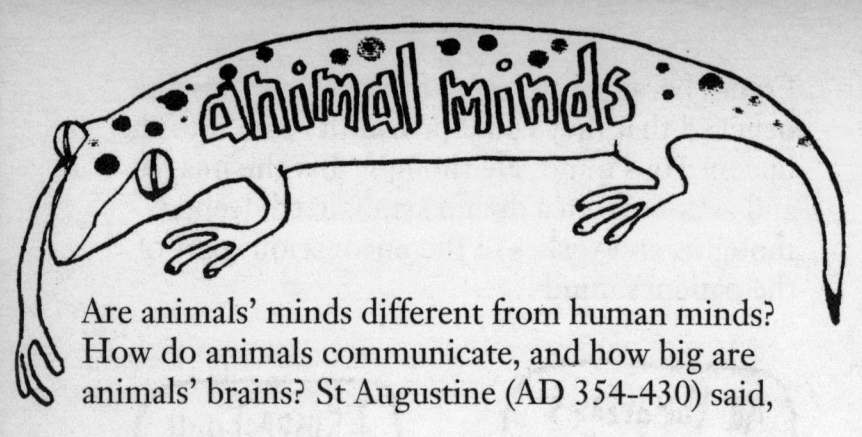

animal minds

Are animals' minds different from human minds? How do animals communicate, and how big are animals' brains? St Augustine (AD 354-430) said,

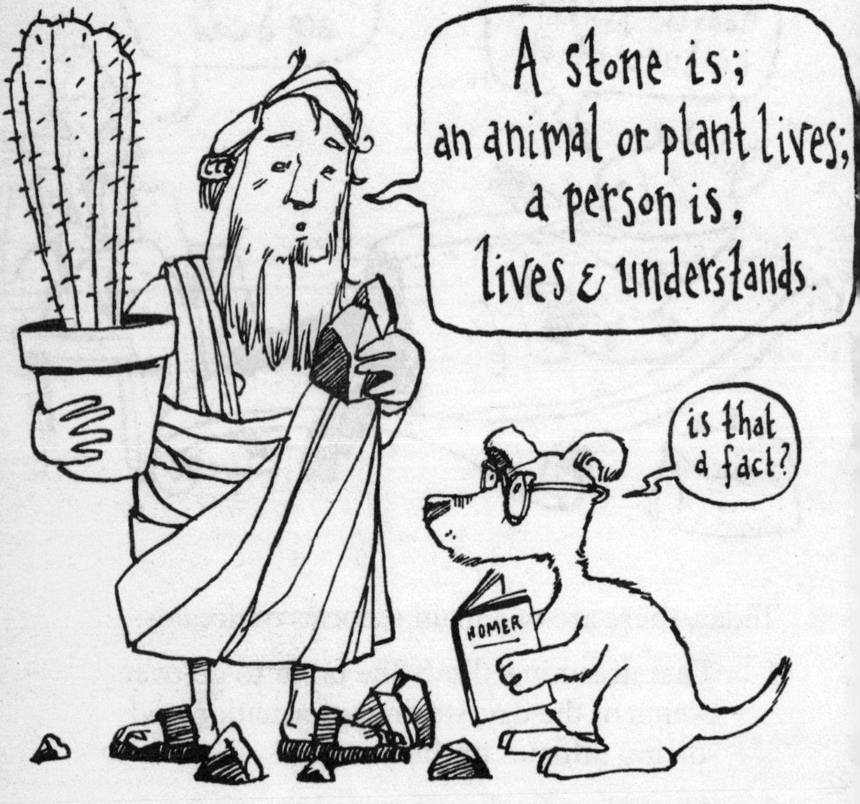

> A stone is;
> an animal or plant lives;
> a person is,
> lives & understands.

is that a fact?

HOMER

Do you agree with St Augustine that only humans actually make sense of the world around them, and that animals live purely by their instincts?

One person who didn't agree with this view, and who changed the way that people thought about animals and humans was Charles Darwin (1809-82). In his books *The Origin of Species* (1859) and *The Descent of Man* (1871) Darwin argued that by the process of evolution, humans are descended from apes … Many people were very insulted to be told that they were related to monkeys!

Since that time, there have been many studies to try to understand animal minds and animal behaviour …

So how does the human brain compare with animal brains? Some whales have brains that are five times as large as the human brain, and elephants have brains four times larger than a human's. But, of course, whales and elephants are huge creatures, so you would expect them to have big brains!

But what about our closer animal relations, the apes? Monkeys and chimps have the biggest brains compared to the size of their bodies of all the animals that live on land. But compared to the weight of the human body, human brains are even bigger than monkey and chimp brains. And not only is the human brain larger in size, but the cortex is more deeply folded and grooved …

One of the main differences between humans and animals is in language. Human language, unlike animal language, uses words and grammar. But of course, animals do communicate in the most amazing ways ...

Bees communicate by dancing! The waggle dance is performed by a bee to tell other bees in the hive where there is food.

Fireflies communicate by light. They have special chemicals in their tails that give off light. They communicate with each other with flashes of different lengths - rather like a complicated morse code!

Whales communicate huge distances by 'singing' to each other through the oceans. In fact, the blue whale makes the loudest noise of any animal - a huge, deep grunt that can travel at least 1500 kilometres …

In the rainforests, birds usually communicate by sound. In order to make the sound travel through the dense blanket of leaves, rainforest birds often have simple, loud calls.
On the flat, open prairie grasslands of America, animals can communicate by sight. If there is danger, the pronghorn antelope flashes a white patch on its rump to warn other animals …

The study of animals continues to reveal countless fascinating facts about animal behaviour. For instance, did you know that animals can use tools?

On one of the Galapagos Islands in the Pacific Ocean, finches use cactus spines or small twigs to force insects out of deep cracks in the rock. The birds hold these tools in their beaks.

Sea otters often carry a stone to help them bash tightly attached shells off rocks. They also use their stone to open the shells up and get at the food inside.

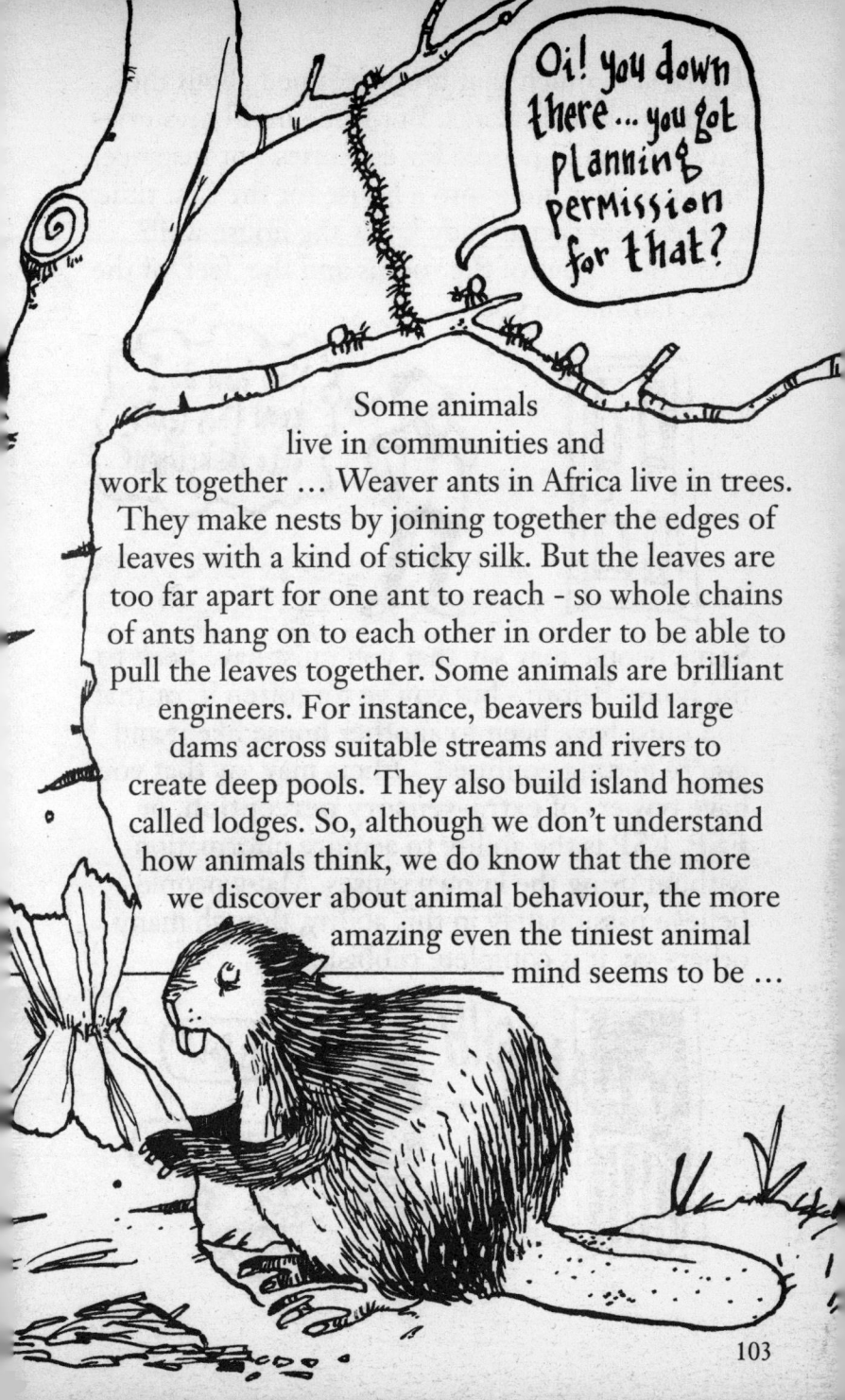

Oi! you down there ... you got planning permission for that?

Some animals live in communities and work together ... Weaver ants in Africa live in trees. They make nests by joining together the edges of leaves with a kind of sticky silk. But the leaves are too far apart for one ant to reach - so whole chains of ants hang on to each other in order to be able to pull the leaves together. Some animals are brilliant engineers. For instance, beavers build large dams across suitable streams and rivers to create deep pools. They also build island homes called lodges. So, although we don't understand how animals think, we do know that the more we discover about animal behaviour, the more amazing even the tiniest animal mind seems to be ...

There is so much that is unexplained about the mind and how it works. But some mind mysteries have fascinated people for centuries. For instance, have you ever gone into a house for the first time and felt that you already knew the house well? Were the layout of the rooms and the 'feel' of the place familiar to you?

Some people may say that you must have been to the house before - but you've forgotten it, or that you must have been to another house like it and you're getting confused. Others may say that you have powers of **extra-sensory perception**, or **ESP**. ESP is the ability to acquire information without using the known senses. Many people believe passionately in this ability, though many others say it is complete rubbish.

People who believe in it say that there are several different kinds of ESP. **Telepathy** is when people claim to be able to communicate through the power of the mind. **Clairvoyance** is when people claim to acquire information that is beyond the range of the senses (for instance, reading the pages of a closed book). **Precognition** is when people claim that they can see what will happen in the future. Some people also claim to be able to move objects without actually touching them, simply by the power of their minds.

The mind is a very powerful thing, but there is little scientific evidence to back all these claims. What do you think?

Can you learn while you are asleep? The obvious answer is 'no'. But some people believe that by playing a tape that repeats the same message throughout the night, your brain will unconsciously 'learn' the information on the tape.

THIS COULD BE A GOOD WAY TO LEARN YOUR HOMEWORK (NOT)

Scientists are not certain about sleep learning. Some believe that it has no effect. Others think that learning could happen during periods of lighter sleep during the night. But it's probably safer to learn your homework during the day!

Advertisers know a lot about the power of the mind.

What has toilet paper got to do with a puppy? Not a lot! But everyone remembers the sweet, soft, cuddly puppy, and as a result they remember the name of the toilet paper too.

Can you think of other examples of adverts that use unusual ways to remember their products?

Our search for the mind has become centred on the workings of the central nervous system inside the human body, particularly the brain. The more we know about the brain, the more complicated it becomes.

In order to try to understand the brain, people have always compared it to the latest and most up-to-date technology.

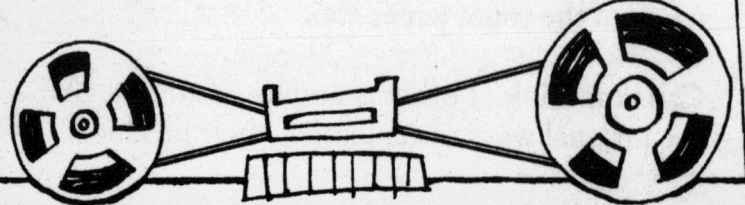

In the 20th century, the brain has been compared to a telephone system, and most often to a computer …

Computers are excellent at calculations and logical processes. A computer program can beat the chess masters of the world because it can explore very quickly the millions of possibilities presented by each move.

But your brain is much, much more complicated than even the most up-to-date computer!

Since the late 1950s, scientists have been trying to make machines that will do tasks which usually require human intelligence. This is called **artificial intelligence**, or AI. Using AI, scientists have developed robots which have proved particularly useful for replacing humans in dangerous situations, such as defusing a bomb or fighting a fire, or repairing a ship underwater …

Another application of A1 is the speech recognition machine. These machines can understand words spoken by a human. Speech recognition machines are already used in airports … in some cars, to turn on radios and heaters … on many telephone answering services … and computer software will now read back to you the words you type on the screen!

In Japan, scientists are developing fuzzy machines! These aren't machines covered in fur, but machines which make fuzzy decisions – more like the decisions made by the human brain than by a computer. Instead of there being a right or wrong answer, there's a 'maybe' programmed into the way the machine works. Fuzzy washing machines analyse the contents of each load and then program themselves. So no more wondering whether to put those socks in a hot wash or not! Let the machine take the strain!

Let's look towards the future of brain research and see which bits of the brain scientists will be studying in the next few years.

The gap between two neurons is called a **synapse**. But what happens as nerve messages jump across this? This tiny gap is providing scientists with lots to think about! When a message reaches the tip of the axon of a neuron, tiny bodies called **vesicles** release chemicals. These chemicals are **neurotransmitters**. The neurotransmitters travel across the synapse to the dendrite of the next neuron.

It is these chemicals, not only inside the brain, but also in the whole of the central nervous system, which are fascinating scientists. They think that even our emotions are the result of chemical changes in the central nervous system …
So next time you fall in love with someone, remember – it's all chemical!

Yet another amazing fact about the brain …
We know that different areas of the brain have
different jobs, but that the brain's interconnectivity
makes sure that all the parts of the brain work
together. Scientists are finding out more about the
adaptability of the brain by studying people who
have had parts of their brains removed.

You've only got half a BRAiN

For some people this is true! Sometimes doctors
remove one of the cerebral hemispheres of the
brain in order to deal with rare brain disorders
which cannot be treated in any other way. Patients
survive these operations because it doesn't affect the
brain stem or the cerebellum.

But the astonishing thing about patients who have had half of their brains removed, is that the 'jobs' of the removed bit are often taken over by the half which remains.

You remember that the two sides of the brain specialize in different things? So someone who has had the left side of their brain removed might be expected not to be very good at music or maths. But quite often, the right side seems to 'learn' these jobs and to make up for the missing bit of the brain …

What do you do if you are ill? Go to the doctor? Take some medicine? Your mind can be a powerful healer – it's just a question of knowing how to use it.

Your body has many different ways of fighting off illness:

If you eat something infected, you will be sick …

If you get something in your eye, tears come out to wash it …

If you graze your knee, the skin mends itself …

Your body is amazing, but people are beginning to realise that the mind is even more astonishing in its power to heal.

Imagine two boys playing football. They injure each other in a tackle. Unfortunately, they both break a leg. One of the boys is determined to get better as quickly as he possibly can, in order to get back on to the football pitch. The other boy is angry and upset about his injury and wonders whether he wants to play football any more.

Which one recovers more quickly?

Well, they might both get better at about the same time – but studies have shown that the boy with the positive attitude is likely to make a faster recovery. The mind influences the body and speeds up the return to fitness! There are many other cases of people recovering from even serious illness through the power and determination of their minds! No one really understands how this works, but the link between a healthy mind and a healthy body seems to be very strong.

So, how can you make the most of your amazing mind? There are whole books written on this subject! But here are a few tips to set you on your way:

BE POSITIVE
Remember our geniuses? They knew how to learn from their mistakes and how to turn them into positive experiences.

I CAN! and I WILL!

BE INQUISITIVE
Remember, you'll never stop learning throughout your whole life, and exploring new worlds and experiences activates the neurons in your brain to greater interconnectivity.

EAT WELL
Your brain can't function properly without good brain food! Make sure you eat lots of vegetables and fruit, and try to avoid too many sweets!

TAKE EXERCISE
A healthy body is as important as a healthy mind.

READ MORE!
If you have found this book interesting – there are lots and lots of other books which will tell you lots more interesting facts about your amazing mind and how to make the most of it. Go to your local library and look in the psychology section, or in the health section. Or ask a librarian for help …

And remember …

"Reading is to the mind what exercise is to the body." (Sir Richard Steele)

THE END

Further reading

Mega Memory by Jonathan Hancock
(Hodder Children's Books)

The Mindmap Book: Radiant Thinking
by Tony Buzan with Barry Buzan (BBC Books)

Use your Head by Tony Buzan (BBC Books)

Buzan's Book of Genius and how to unleash your own
by Tony Buzan and Raymond Keene
(Stanley Paul)

The Mind Machine by Colin Blakemore
(Penguin/BBC Books)

Jung for Beginners by Maggie Hyde and Michael
McGuinness (Icon Books)

Freud for Beginners by Richard Appignanesi and
Oscar Zarate (Icon Books)

The Brain and Nervous System
by Steve Parker (Watts)

The Oxford Companion to the Mind
by Richard Gregory (OUP)

Edward de Bono's Mind Pack
(Dorling Kindersley)

Great Minds in the History of the Mind

Hippocrates (460-370BC) Often known as the Father of Medicine – he said that all diseases have natural causes rather than being the work of the gods!

Plato (427-347BC) He founded an Academy in Athens – a kind of school of advanced learning. He was very concerned with the 'psyche', the 'living self', and its many different parts.

Aristotle (384-322BC) Studied with Plato at his Academy. He said that the function of the brain was to cool the blood when it became too hot. He said that the mind ('soul') was a part of the body.

St Augustine (AD354-430) Bishop of Hippo, North Africa. He said that the 'soul' ('mind') leaves the body after death and becomes immortal.

St Thomas Aquinas (1224/5-1274) He taught at the universities of Paris and Naples. He went back to Aristotle for his ideas, but he said that some things can only be learned through the Christian faith.

Thomas Hobbes (1588-1679) He was born prematurely because of his mother's terror when she heard of the arrival of the Spanish Armada. He put the mind and body together, and said that everything in the mind arises from experience.

René Descartes (1596-1650) Lived for much of his life in Holland, but in 1649 went to Sweden to teach Queen Christina philosophy and died of a cold. He separated the body and the mind, saying that during life they were joined by a small gland in the brain.

John Locke (1632-1704) Educated at Westminster School in London and Oxford. He used the word 'idea' to describe the things that the mind thinks about. He said that all ideas come from sensation and reflection.

Immanuel Kant (1724-1804) He was born in Könisberg in Prussia (present-day Kaliningrad in Russia) and taught at the University there. He never travelled more than a few kilometres from the city in the whole of his life. He said that the human mind not only learned from experience, but also has the power of intuition.

Wilhelm Wundt (1832-1920) He founded the Institute for Experimental Psychology in Leipzig, the first laboratory dedicated to the study of psychology. He is considered by many people to be the father of modern psychology. He studied the processes of the mind through experiment.

William James (1842-1910) Brother of novelist Henry James. He was a teacher at Harvard University. He introduced psychology to the USA. He once said, 'The first lecture in psychology that I ever heard was the first I ever gave.'

Ivan Pavlov (1849-1936) He studied medicine and became a professor at St Petersburg University. He is famous for his research on dogs which led to the discovery of the 'conditioned reflex'.

Sigmund Freud (1856-1939) Probably the most

famous figure in the history of psychology. He worked in Vienna, Austria. He invented psychoanalysis – the process of studying the workings of the unconscious mind.

Carl Jung (1875-1961) A colleague of Freud's, but he split away from Freud and his ideas to develop his own theories. Jung tried to place humans in a universal, historical context. He called his approach analytical psychology.

John B. Watson (1878-1958) He founded an American school of psychology called behaviourism. The aim of his school was to try to understand the mind through the study of behaviour.

Wolfgang Köhler (1887-1967) Together with Max Wertheimer and Kurt Koffka he founded the school of Gestaltists. 'Gestalt' means 'whole' or 'pattern', and the Gestalt school developed the idea that the brain works on information from the senses to make sense of a whole picture

Jean Piaget (1896-1980) A Swiss psychologist who devoted his life to the study of children. Through observation and experiment he investigated the way children learn and develop.

B.F. Skinner (1904-1990) A member of the behaviourist school. He showed that behaviour that is rewarded is likely to be repeated. This is called operant behaviour.

Glossary

AI (Artificial Intelligence) the science of machines which will do tasks that normally require human intelligence.

Alzheimer's disease a disease that attacks the brain. People with Alzheimer's lose their memory, and their ability to communicate.

Central nervous system the brain and the spinal cord.

Conscious the bit of the mind we use all the time to think, to make decisions, to speak.

Dissection the practice of cutting up plants or animals for scientific research.

EEG (electroencephalography) a way of measuring the tiny electrical messages in your brain. These electrical signals are shown on a screen or a paper chart as wavy lines.

Emotion a strong feeling such as love or hate.

ESP (extra-sensory perception) the ability to aquire information without using the known senses.

Hypnosis a trance-like state in which a person has no control over their words or behaviour on a conscious level, but in which they are open to suggestion at an unconscious level.

IQ (Intelligence Quotient) a way of measuring intelligence developed in the 20th century.

Memory the part of the brain that stores and retrieves information.

Mental describes anything to do with the mind.

Mnemonic a device to help memory storage and retrieval.

Neuron the name for the nerve cells that make up your central nervous system.

Neuroscience the study of the brain.

Optical illusion something that deceives the eye.

Personality the way a person is and behaves.

Phobia an irrational fear of an object or situation.

Phrenology the science that claimed to be able to distinguish character traits by the shape of lumps in the skull.

Psychiatry the branch of medicine that is concerned with the care and treatment of people with illnesses of the mind.

Psychology the study of the mind.

Schizophrenia an illness that has many different symptoms. People suffering from schizophrenia hear voices, behave in odd ways that they cannot explain, jumble up their words and thoughts.

Trepanation the practice of cutting a hole in the skull.

Unconscious the automatic or hidden parts of the brain that control all sorts of systems in your body without your being aware of it.

Index

Alzheimer's disease   37, 47
amygdala   16, 51, 87
Ancient Egyptians   10
Ancient Greeks   11, 50
animals   29, 77, 96-100, 101-103
artificial intelligence   110, 111
axon   19, 112
babies   15, 72, 73, 81, 88
brain   10-23, 25-30, 33- 39, 41, 47, 49-53, 58, 59, 63-70, 72, 73, 78-81, 87, 92, 93, 96, 98, 99, 108, 109, 111-115
brain stem   17, 27, 114
breathing   24
central nervous system   13, 14, 18, 28, 29, 108, 113
cerebellum   115
cerebrum   17, 22
clairvoyance   105
conscious   41, 44
connectivity   19, 73, 81, 118
corpus callosum   16, 23
cortex   16, 20, 22, 37, 63, 99
    motor   20
    sensory   20
creativity   22, 85
Darwin, Charles (1809-1882)   97
dendrite   18, 19, 112
depression   47
Descartes, René (1596-1650)   12, 76
digestion   24
dissection   31
dreams   93- 95
Einstein, Albert (1879-1955)   80
electroencephalography 37
emotions   11, 35, 47, 53, 86-89, 113

evolution   97
extra-sensory perception   104, 105
eyes   32, 33, 62-64, 73, 93
Freud, Sigmund (1856-1939)   41, 59, 95
Gage, Phineas   34, 35
genius   80, 82- 85, 118
Gall, Franz Joseph (1758-1828)   32,33
head   10, 35, 59
heart   10-12, 24, 93
hemispheres   22, 23, 114
hippocampus   16, 37, 51
Hippocrates (460-370BC)   11
hypnosis   42-45
hypothalamus   17, 24, 25, 87
intelligence   9, 15, 80-82, 84, 85
IQ   84, 85
language   76, 77
learning   48, 70-77, 80, 81, 106
logic   22, 85
maths   22, 23, 85, 115
medulla   16
mental illness   38, 39, 47
Mensa   84
memory   9, 11, 29, 32, 33, 37, 45, 48-52, 54-56, 58, 59, 70, 71, 76, 107
    long-term   52
    short-term   53
Mesmer, Dr Franz Anton (1734-1815)   42, 43
mesmerism   43
mnemonic   56, 57
muscles   20, 21, 25
nerves   14, 18, 19, 23
neurons (nerve cells)   15, 18, 19, 28, 29, 37, 51, 59, 72, 81, 112, 118
neurotransmitters   112
neuroscience   13

nuclear magnetic
  resonance 36
nucleus 18
optical illusions 68, 69
personality 89-91
philosophers 12
phobias 40, 41, 47
phrenology 33
Piaget, Jean
  (1896-1980) 74, 75
pons 16
positive attitude 117
positron-emission
  tomography 36
precognition 105
psychiatry 30, 47
psychology 30, 46, 47,
119
psychotherapy 47
puzzles 22, 23, 68
reading 22, 26, 78,
79, 119
recognition 22, 73-75
repression 59
reticular formation 17, 27
Rorschach, Hermann 90
schizophrenia 47

senses 14, 60, 61,
63
  hearing 53, 73
  sight 20
  taste 53
skull 14, 16, 31,
33, 34
sleep 29, 37, 92,
93, 106
speech 22, 46, 48,
76, 78
spinal cord 14, 17, 18,
27, 28
soul 12
synapse 112
telepathy 105
thalamus 17
trepanation 31
unconscious 41, 44, 45,
95
Vesalius, Andreas
  (1514-1564) 31
vesicles 112
da Vinci, Leonardo
  (1472-1519) 31
writing 22, 76, 78
x-ray 36